JONAH
A Study
in Compassion

∾∾∾∾∾∾∾∾

O. PALMER ROBERTSON

G000166653

THE BANNER OF TRUTH TRUST

THE BANNER OF TRUTH TRUST
3 Murrayfield Road, Edinburgh EH12 6EL
PO Box 621, Carlisle, Pennsylvania 17013, USA

*

© O. Palmer Robertson 1990
First published 1990
ISBN 0 85151 575 4

*

Set in 11/12pt Linotron Times
Typeset at The Spartan Press Ltd,
Lymington, Hants
and printed and bound in Great Britain by
BPCC Hazell Books
Aylesbury, Bucks, England
Member of BPCC Ltd.

Contents

DEDICATED TO THE MEMBERS AND FRIENDS

OF WALLACE MEMORIAL PRESBYTERIAN CHURCH

WHOSE LOVE OF THE LORD

AND VISION FOR MISSIONS

HAS DONE SO MUCH TO INSPIRE THESE MESSAGES.

IN FLIGHT

(Jonah 1:1, 2)

If you have a flight simulator for your computer, you know that crashing an airplane is a fairly easy thing to do. Just dip your nose a little too low, and you will find how quickly the ground comes up to meet you.

Living your life in relation to God's will may be regarded as a form of flying. A sinner is a lot like a bumblebee: he isn't supposed to fly. Too many things tend to pull him down from a walk with God. Past patterns of life urge him to go with the flow of a corrupt culture. Loyalties to family, to an ethnic community, to a political system tug him toward doing things that identify him as something other than a stranger and a pilgrim with God who has no continuing city in this world.

Jonah faced these tensions, and he responded by taking off. He fled in order to escape from doing the will of God.

What about you? Are you right now at the point in your life where you are fairly sure what God wants you to do, but you are 'on the run'? Are you deliberately fooling yourself, using God's invisibility as a cover for not doing what you know you ought to do? Follow closely the path of Jonah to see if perhaps you should make some critical corrections on your present course.

'Now the word of the Lord came to Jonah' (*Jon. 1:1*).

Such a momentous event should not be taken for granted. Shortly after Jonah's day, another prophet predicted a famine. But it would be a very distinctive famine. Not a famine of bread or of water, but a famine of hearing the word of God (*Amos 8:11*).

It would be far better to starve to death with your heart filled with the word of God than to be stuffed with food and be empty in your soul. The psalmist says that because of Israel's constant complaining about their diet, the Lord gave them what they wanted, but sent leanness into their souls (*Psa. 106:15*).

Jonah was privileged beyond measure because the word of the Lord came to him. But you are even more privileged. You know from the incarnate Word of God where to find salvation and how to live your life. Be sure you recognize fully your privilege in knowing the will of God for your life. His will is not something to dread; it is the way to fulness in life.

This was not the first time that the word of the Lord came to Jonah. Earlier he had been given the privilege of announcing great blessing for the people of God, even though they did not deserve it. The narrative is found in II Kings 14:24–27 where we read of Jeroboam II, who ruled over the northern kingdom of Israel from about 783 to 743 B.C.:

24 He did evil in the eyes of the Lord and did not turn away from any of the sins of Jeroboam son of Nebat, which he had caused Israel to commit.

25 [Jeroboam II] was the one who restored the boundaries of Israel from Lebo Hamath to the Sea

of the Arabah, in accordance with the word of the Lord, the God of Israel, spoken through his servant Jonah son of Amittai, the prophet from Gath Hepher.

26 The Lord had seen how bitterly everyone in Israel, whether slave or free, was suffering; there was no one to help them.

27 And since the Lord had not said he would blot out the name of Israel from under heaven, he saved them by the hand of Jeroboam son of Jehoash.

Jeroboam was a very wicked king. Yet through Jonah came a word of mercy and grace. The land-holdings of Israel would be expanded back to the era of prosperity under Solomon.

'This church is going to grow and grow and grow! The membership's going to double, the blessings will abound, and everybody will enjoy prosperity.' It would be a pleasant task to announce that kind of message as the word of the Lord. That was Jonah's first prophetic assignment.

This blessing would come on the people because of the Lord's compassion for them, not particularly for their repentance from sin. They were loved of God, and in his grace he would bless them in spite of their sin.

Now comes a new word for Jonah to announce. Can you imagine his excitement as he senses that the word of the Lord is coming once more? He had been very concerned about the absence of repentance among the people. They continued in their idolatrous worship. The goodness of God that should have led them to repentance only fostered more selfishness and greed. All people could think about was more money, political power and pleasure.

'What will the Lord say now?', Jonah might have thought. Would he increase his blessings on Israel even more as a way of making them recognize the goodness of God? Or would it now become the difficult task of Jonah to announce that the Lord would have to begin chastening them for their sin as a way of bringing them to repentance?

'Jonah,' says the voice of the Lord, 'Pack your Bible and your bags. I want you to take the next boat to Nineveh, the capital of Assyria. There you must preach against that city, because its wickedness has come up to me' (*Jon. 1:2*).

It took a moment for Jonah to absorb this new set of directions. What was this all about? He was a home-town boy from Amittai. He never had been out of his home state, much less the country. Now he was to get a passport, go through customs, and take an international trip to that massive metropolis of Nineveh? What did all this mean?

You know Jonah's reaction. He began to flee. But do you know why he fled?

Jonah did not resist doing the will of God because he was afraid of travelling to a foreign country. His self-chosen destination of Tarshish was a far more distant place than Nineveh.

Did Jonah flee because he was embarrassed to stand on the street corner and look like a fool preaching to the passers-by? No, it was nothing so trite as that.

Incidentally, if something like fear of what people might think of you is keeping you from

[10]

doing the will of God, then shame on you. Pray that with all boldness the Lord will give you courage to speak his word wherever and whenever he directs.

Some have suggested that Jonah fled because he did not want to prophesy something that might not come to pass. How red-faced he would be if he prophesied the doom of Nineveh and then the Lord spared them in his mercy. But that explanation for Jonah's flight from the will of God seems silly. Jonah was no ignoramus with respect to the purposes of God. He understood God's mercy. He knew that a prophetic announcement of doom left the possibility of mercy in the event of repentance. Why would he have been embarrassed if his preaching was effective enough to bring the heathen Ninevites to their knees?

That, as a matter of fact, was just the thing that was troubling Jonah. It took him a few minutes to put the whole scenario together. But what he saw he did not like at all.

Suppose he should leave his beloved land of Israel and travel to the heathen city of Nineveh. Suppose he should there preach the coming judgment of God: 'Within forty days your city shall be wiped out for its wickedness.' The Ninevites might be struck in their consciences because of the obvious truthfulness of his denunciations. They would then cry out to the Lord for mercy and forgiveness; and the Lord would show his wonderful compassion to them. He would forgive them, and embrace them in his favour. They would be claimed in God's mercy as his sons who had returned home.

'That's it!' says Jonah. 'It has to be. There's no other reason the Lord would be sending me on this long journey outside the borders of Israel. Why otherwise would he bother with these depraved heathen? Hundreds of nations have crumbled because of their sin without a specific word from a prophet of the Lord. Prophets are for God's people. So if I'm being sent to Nineveh, the Lord must be intending to claim them as his adopted sons, just as he once claimed the clan of Abraham.'

So far so good.

You can take heart from Jonah's experience in preaching to strangers you do not know. If God lays a certain people on your heart, it may be an indicator that he intends to lead them to repentance and faith through you. When it becomes your task to declare to someone his sin against God, rejoice! Do not run! It may be God's first step in bringing them to himself, as hard as it might be for you.

But why did Jonah run? Why should he not rejoice in the salvation of the heathen?

To answer that question, you must take the logic one more step. Jonah already had preached to Israel, and they had not repented. He had not been the first prophet sent to Israel. For one hundred and fifty years, God had been sending his servants the prophets. They had denounced the idolatry of Israel in no uncertain terms.

But Israel had rejected their message. For one hundred and fifty years they had persisted in their sinful ways.

So now what does his mission to Nineveh mean? Could it mean that the centre of gravity for God's working in the world might shift from Israel to Assyria? If that heathen nation turns to the Lord at his preaching, what would that imply for the future relations between a repentant Assyria and an unrepentant Israel?

Do you get the picture? The relation of men and nations to the Lord is dynamic, not static. God does not go by the status quo. Remember what Paul says to the Gentiles who had been blessed by faith in the Lord? They had been grafted into the stock of Israel. By grace they had become a bona fide part of the people of God (*Rom. 11:17*). The Gentiles had been under the curse of God, but now they had become God's people.

But they too could be cut off again (*Rom. 11:21*). Even as Israel had been cut off, so the Gentiles who had been grafted into Christ could be cut off. If they as a people did not continue in faith, they could be removed from the blessings of Christ.

So Jonah ran. He fled because he wanted to protect his people. He would rather see the heathen Ninevites perish than see the disobedient Israelites perish. Assyria would be the natural instrument in God's hand to bring judgment on Israel. If they now became favourably identified with the Lord, what would be left to hinder their becoming the tool in the Lord's hands to wipe out Israel?

Jonah was not too far from the truth. Within twenty years of the end of Jeroboam II's rule, the Assyrians came down and devastated Israel. They carried into captivity the cream of the youth of the northern nation.

Was Jonah right to run? Of course he was not right. How can man presume to tell God how to run the affairs of the world? If God wants to save the heathen and bring judgment on those who have

[13]

previously received his favours, that is his right. The Lord of all the earth shall do right.

What about today? The word of the Lord has come to you. It has come just as plainly as it came to Jonah. The Lord says you are to go to the great cities of the world. You are to go and preach against them, for their wickedness has come before the Lord. Go and denounce corruption in politics, in business, in morals. Go expecting that in the mercy of the Lord people may come to repentance and faith in the Lord Jesus Christ. Go with an understanding that all the things precious to you may be lost in the process. Go with a readiness to sacrifice your time-honoured traditions.

Are you 'in flight'? Is your church 'in flight'? Is your commitment to the maintenance of your traditions higher than your commitment to fulfil the great commission? The church's commission from God includes the suburbs. But that is not all. Your commission also includes the cities.

Stop running from the Lord. Lift up your eyes to the fields, for they are white already to the harvest.

IN PURSUIT
(Jonah 1:3–16)

Jonah is in flight. But God is in pursuit. It is a futile flight, and it is a persistent pursuit.

Francis Thompson, the British poet of the turn of the century, writes of 'The Hound of Heaven'. In his epic poem, he describes God's undaunted pursuit of the man who flees him:

> *I fled Him, down the nights and down the days;*
> *I fled Him, down the arches of the years;*
> *I fled Him, down the labyrinthine ways*
> *Of my own mind; and in the mist of tears*
> *I hid from Him, and under running laughter.*
>   *Up vistaed hopes I sped;*
>   *And shot, precipitated,*
> *Adown Titanic glooms of chasmed fears,*
>   *From those strong feet that followed,*
>   *followed after.*
>   *But with unhurrying chase,*
>   *And unperturbed pace,*
> *Deliberate speed, majestic instancy,*
>   *They beat-and a Voice beat*
>   *More instant than the Feet –*
> *'All things betray thee, who betrayest Me.'*

And again:
'Naught shelters thee, who wilt not shelter Me.'

And again:

'Lo! naught contents thee, who content'st not Me.'

And in the end:

'All which I took from thee I did but take,
*   Not for thy harms,*
But just that thou might'st seek it in my arms.
*   All which thy child's mistake*
Fancies as lost, I have stored for thee at home:
*   Rise, clasp My hand, and come!'[1]*

Life never stands still. Either you are running with the will of God, or you are fleeing from the will of God. Time puts you on the move, and you cannot stop. Every day you become more in the image of God, or you regress from that image.

'Jonah rose up to flee to Tarshish from the face of Jahweh' (*Jon. 1:3a*).

It seems so silly, but you do it constantly. Trying to get away from God is like trying to get away from air. In him we live and move and have our being.

Surely for the person in covenant with God it is utter folly to try to flee from him. God never will let you out of his sight. He has determined to bless you, and he will keep after you until he overruns you with the blessing he intends.

'And he went down to Joppa and found a boat going to Tarshish; and he paid the fare to go with them to Tarshish from the face of Jahweh' (Jon. 1:3b).

Providential provision, was it not? How else could you read the circumstances? It probably was

[1]*Modern British Poetry*, ed. Louis Untermeyer, 1950, pp. 86–90.

not the time of year for sailing on the Mediterranean Sea. Yet Jonah easily finds a ship ready to sail. Furthermore, ships sailing to Tarshish must have been as rare as direct flights to Juno. Tarshish was at the utter end of the earth as known in Jonah's day. Spain it was. Yet he hardly walks onto Joppa dock before he finds a boat ready to go.

But the clincher was the fare. Jonah had just the right amount of money to book his passage. It was amazing enough when he discovered that they still had a cabin open. But when he learned that he could afford the fare, he knew it must be providential. He had rushed out of Gath Hepher with hardly the time to get his money from the bank. If it had not been for the twenty-four hour teller, he really would have been in trouble. But now everything was set.

Sometimes when everything is going just right, you conclude that God's hand must be in it. But that may not be the case at all. You need something more specific than circumstances. You need the confirmation of the word of God.

How many times in your life have you gone against the teaching of the word of God because you had tunnel vision and stubbornly saw only what you wanted? Beware of reading providential circumstances in a way that contradicts the explicit commands of the Lord.

'But Jahweh hurled a great wind on the sea, and there was a mighty tempest in the sea, and the ship was threatening to be broken apart' (*Jon. 1:4*).

What did the Lord do with this great wind? He 'hurled' it. Insurance companies are not far off when they describe the damage done by a tropical storm as an 'act of God'. But Scripture is even more specific. With this storm God took aim on 'Target Jonah' and hurled his tempest with unerring accuracy. Elsewhere in the Bible this word describes what a man does with a javelin. He takes careful aim at his chosen target, and with all his strength he 'hurls' his chosen weapon.

Jonah's ship is the Lord's target. This man cannot possibly escape. The God of the covenant is in hot pursuit.

There is no place where you can hide from God. He has at his disposal all the forces of the universe, and summons them to do his bidding as he will.

'The sailors were terrified and they cried each man to his god. They even cast forth the cargo which was in the boat into the sea, to lighten it' (*Jon. 1:5a*).

The heathen are particularly fearful of natural phenomena. They are much like the great German shepherd dog trembling under the bed at the sound of thunder. Nature is god to the heathen. They have no higher power to which they can appeal. The instinct for survival leads these sailors spontaneously to pour into the sea all their treasures.

Jonah's sin was of the most private sort. He alone knew of his sin against the will of God for his life.

But his action had sad consequences for these sailors as well as for himself. They lost all their cargo, and now their lives were threatened. God had offered Jonah the privilege of blessing the whole populace of the great city of Nineveh, but he became a curse to a few unsuspecting sailors instead.

You will invariably bring trouble to the life of

others as well as to your own life if you are walking contrary to the will of God. Christians who work with prisoners will tell you that the story of Jonah always captures the attention of people in jail. They know they are running from God. They understand what it means to hurt other people, especially the ones they love, by going against God's will.

Don't be a dog in the manger. Don't be a curse to everybody you contact. Give yourself to the doing of the will of God.

'But Jonah had gone down into the hold of the ship, where he lay down and fell asleep' (*Jon. 1:5b*).

What a peaceful scene. Jonah is snoring so loudly that he can't even hear the raging of the wind on deck above. The trip to Joppa had totally worn him out. The evident providential goodness of the Lord had put his mind completely at rest. He was Tarshish-bound, his people were safe, and he could forget all about the threat of Assyria against Israel. Obviously the Lord would not use them as his instrument to chastise Israel so long as they continued in their wicked ways. He hated to run out on an assignment from the Lord, but everything was working out fine. Jonah had peace in his heart.

Beware of overplaying the significance of feelings. Ahab felt exhilarated when he first claimed Naboth's property, until he met Elijah. Saul felt great as he offered the sacrifices before battle, until he met Samuel. Herod felt quite content taking his brother's wife until he met John the Baptist. Do not assume that fickle feelings determine whether or not you are doing the will of God.

Do you realize how subtle words can be? Very often a phrase comes to mean the exact opposite of what it actually says. I have seen Christians shatter the terms of a contract, and cover over their action by stating, 'I really do feel good about it.' In this case, 'I really feel good about it' actually means, 'I have suppressed my conscience on this matter.'

Sometimes the name of God is blasphemed by the most pious Christians. Have you ever heard the phrase, 'I just didn't feel the Lord wanted me to do it,' or 'I really didn't have peace in that matter'? Well-intended Christians will break their word to you and cover infidelity with a cloak of 'feeling'.

Jonah had plenty of peace. He was sleeping like a baby. At the very time when he was running from the will of God, he had great peace.

Beware of appeals to inner peace. Listen to what the word of God teaches, and let it be your guide to life.

Yet a deeply settling peace will belong to those who busy themselves with doing the will of God. The New Testament tells of a 'greater than Jonah' who also slept in the hold of a ship in the midst of a storm. He was utterly exhausted from all the labours of the day. The multitudes pressed him with their unending needs. When he went into his friend Peter's house to get a little relief, there was the mother-in-law lying in bed tormented with a fever, needing his attention. Even into the evening the steady stream continued as they brought to the door all those that had illnesses. He literally fulfilled the prophecy of Isaiah, 'He took into himself our infirmities, and bore the burden of our diseases' (*Mt. 8:16, 17*).

No wonder Jesus slept soundly despite the storm

on the sea of Galilee. But the disciples were in a panic. They frantically aroused him, and he stilled the storm.

You need not have the elements fighting against you. Why be of little faith? Accept the commands of God that come to you as being for your best and for the best of the world in which you live. Then you can share Christ's mission of being a blessing to the world rather than bringing trouble to the world.

'The captain went to him and said, "How can you sleep? Get up and call on your god! Maybe he will take notice of us, and we will not perish"' (*Jon. 1:6*).

Even the heathen will recognize the reality of the Lord when the going gets rough. These tough heathen sailors fell on their knees.

G. Gordon Liddy wrote his autobiography under the title *Will*. Because he feared heights and electricity as a child, he forced himself to climb to the top of electrical poles. Because he feared rats, he forced himself to kill and eat one. He joined Nietzsche in affirming the will to power as the highest of human goals. He received without flinching a sentence of 21 years in prison because of his participation in the Watergate affair under the administration of President Richard Nixon. But when he began to think of eternity, his iron will crumbled, and he turned to Christ.[2]

'Then the sailors said to each other, "Come, let us cast lots to find out who is responsible for this calamity." They cast lots and the lot fell on Jonah' (*Jon. 1:7*).

[2](*Christianity Today*, Sept. 2, 1988, p. 72).

Can you imagine Jonah's complacency? The boat is heaving its last. The cargo has been dumped. The captain has become religious, and the seasoned sailors are desperate. Jonah knows exactly who is to blame, but he doesn't say a word. His testimony ultimately was a good one, but he certainly was slow in getting it out.

Do not wait until you are forced to testify for Christ before you open your mouth. You have been commanded to be on the aggressive, seeking out opportunities to tell about Christ. Pray with the Apostle Paul that with all boldness you may testify to the grace of Christ, not being intimidated by men.

'So they asked him, "Tell us, who is responsible for making all this trouble for us? What do you do? Where do you come from? What is your country? From what people are you?"' (*Jon. 1:8*).

The lot had fallen on Jonah. He was forced to admit that his game was up.

The sailors show a great deal of common grace. Even though the lot had pointed to Jonah, they give him the benefit of the doubt. Who is responsible?, they ask Jonah. Maybe the lot only means that you know something. They ply him with questions, shooting in the dark, trying somehow to peer into the mystery of God's harsh dealing with them.

'He answered, "I am a Hebrew and I worship Jahweh, the God of heaven, who made the sea and the land"' (*Jon. 1:9*).

Talk about a shocker to the sailors! They were trying to find out which local deity they had offended. But Jonah tells them it is the big One, the one true God of gods that every man knows by the testimony of his heart.

Heaven, sea and land Jonah mentions. See the howling heavens swirling about you? My God made them, he says. Feel the sea heaving under your feet? My God made it. Sense the presence of the rocky coast ahead, where you soon may crash? My God made it.

'This terrified them. They asked, "What have you done?" (They knew he was running away from Jahweh, because he already had told them)' (*Jon. 1:10*).

Jonah's words had the ring of truth. The sailors could not argue with him.

If you will be bold, you may find the mightiest of men trembling before the living God. If you will only speak out, you will find it to be true that his word is like a sharp sword, a discerner of the thoughts and intents of the heart.

How low has Jonah sunk. Rather than glorifying the name of the one true living God before the entire metropolis of Nineveh, he has caused the shaming of the name of Jahweh by telling a few coarse sailors he has been running from him, implying that his God was as limited as theirs.

'So they asked him, "What should we do to you to make the sea calm down for us?" For the sea was heaving and churning' (*Jon. 1:11*).

Jonah has created a 'him' and 'us' situation by his disobedience. All in the ship should have been united in facing the storm. But Jonah's sin has alienated him from the crew. Often when you fail to share Christ, you will eventually see an animosity build up between yourself and the non-

Christian. If you wait too late, your testimony can go unheeded.

'"Pick me up and throw me into the sea," he replied, "and it will become calm for you. For I am absolutely certain that it is because of me that this great storm has come on you"' (*Jon. 1:12*).

What a hard thing to admit. He is to blame for their calamity. Now he must bear the judgment of God for his own sin that they may be spared in their innocence.

Do you see the total contrast with the one greater than Jonah? Rather than creating trouble for others, Christ bore the judgment of God for sinners. But Jonah brought calamity on needy sinners by his own rebellion. What a sad gospel Jonah preached – all because he was determined that his will would prevail over the Lord's.

Bring your life into conformity with the will of God. By the power of the resurrected Christ within you, transform your entire life-style. Begin with the introduction of the little graces like compassion for the lost, humility and a willingness to serve. Show these attitudes to all men without discrimination. Then you will be setting the right context for the true testimony of the gospel.

'Instead, the men rowed with all their might to return the ship to the land, but they could not; for the sea continued to heave and churn against them' (*Jon. 1:13*).

Do you get the irony of the picture? These heathen men show compassion toward Jonah! He, the believer, closes his heart toward the massive metropolis of Nineveh. Although his people had

[24]

experienced the grace of God for generations, he closes his heart to another people. But in dramatic contrast these coarse sailors do everything they can to spare the life of Jonah, even after he has caused the loss of all their cargo, and now may cause their loss of life.

Isn't it disgraceful? Don't you often find more kindness and considerateness among unbelievers than among Christians? Believers bite and devour one another! What a shame and a disgrace.

'Then they cried to Jahweh: 'Ahh, Jahweh''' (*Jon. 1:14a*).

Now these rough sailors do something they have never done before. They earnestly call on God by a name with which their lips are unfamiliar. They use a word for God that is different from the term employed by the captain of the ship earlier (*cf. Jon. 1:6*). 'Cry to your god,' he had said, not knowing one deity from another. But now the sailors cry to Jahweh, the covenant God of the Bible. They believe Jonah. His god is the God of heaven, earth and the sea. 'Ahh, Jahweh,' they exclaim. They give honest expression to the agony of their soul.

Do you understand that there is no other name under heaven by which men may be saved other than the name 'Jesus'? (*Acts 4:12*). Don't be intimidated by the scornful attitudes of people who would neutralize the saving power of the name of Jesus by lowering it to the level of other 'gods'. He alone is Lord of heaven, earth and sea. He alone actually can and actually does save sinners for time and eternity.

'"Do not let us perish for the life of this man, and

do not reckon to our account innocent blood. For you, Lord, have done as you pleased." So they lifted up Jonah and threw him into the sea, and the sea ceased from its raging' (*Jon. 1:14b, 15*).

See how the heathen show more conscience before God than the religious. 'His blood be on our hands, and on the hands of our children,' cried the Jews at the time of the crucifixion of Christ (*Matt. 27:25*). But these men really believe that God avenges innocent blood. With fear and trembling they cast Jonah overboard. The rightness of their act is confirmed immediately by the calming of the sea.

'Then the men were stunned with the fear of Jahweh, and they offered a sacrifice to Jahweh, making solemn commitments' (*Jon. 1:16*).

If only Jonah could be on deck now! He had run to the ends of the earth to avoid seeing the heathen converted. And what does he get as a result? He gets heathen converted. What's more, he gets sailors travelling to the uttermost part of the earth, taking with them the gospel that 'Salvation is of the Lord'. All the way to Spain, a far greater distance than Nineveh, the gospel travels. These sailors may have been the very ones that prepared the way for the spread of the gospel of the new covenant to the farthest extremes of the Gentile world. Some hundreds of years later we read of Paul the Apostle's determination to get to Spain – read Tarshish – with Rome in his estimation being only an intermediate stopping-point along the way (*cf. Rom. 15:24*).

So what do you learn from Jonah's flight and the Lord's pursuit? You learn that God pursues one man to the death that he might bless the many.

[26]

God's grace has a persistence that exceeds all human determinations. God hounds Jonah to the ends of the earth that he might bless the nations.

Jesus – the one described as 'greater than Jonah' – displays the love of God that saves sinners even more clearly. God pursued his own Son even to the death that many from every nation under heaven might be saved.

The Hound of Heaven concludes its description of the divine pursuit:

> *Halts by me that footfall:*
> *Is my gloom, after all,*
> *Shade of His hand, outstretched caressingly?*
> *'Ah, fondest, blindest, weakest,*
> *I am He whom thou seekest!*
> *Thou dravest love from thee, who dravest Me.'*

It is not an evil you are escaping when you flee from the will of God. His will for those who trust him always is an embodiment of his perfect love.

Stop running from God. Give yourself now to the doing of his will.

3

UP FROM THE ABYSS
(Jonah 1:17–2:10)

The sinner goes down. He begins the descent by his own acts of folly. He tries to run from the will of God, and he trips on his own dangling shoelaces. It is just a fact: nothing can be in its right order when you are living in rebellion against the will of God.

The sinner goes down a further step when the Lord begins to chasten him. Jonah went down to Joppa, down into the ship's hold, and down into the belly of the great fish.

You will go down too if you walk out of harmony with the will of God. The circumstances of life will bring you down. Your own inner spirit will bring you down. The hand of the Lord will bring you down.

But rejoice in the grace of our God! For those who are his own, even the downward movement manifests the good intent of God. Joseph went down into the pit, down into slavery, down into Egypt, and down into the dungeon, because God meant it for good, to save many people from many nations alive during the great famine.

The same principle reaches its fullest expression with the descent of Jesus into the abyss. He cried in agony, 'My God, my God, why have you forsaken me?' But a short time later he could say with relief, 'It is finished.' From the cross he descended into the tomb. But from there he rose in glory to reign at the right hand of the Father.

Identify with the experience of Jonah. His was a discovery of the power of the resurrection. He came 'up from the abyss'.

'The Lord had prepared a great fish' (*Jon. 1:17a*).

Do you think it just happened that this massive creature of the deep was treading water in the storm, waiting with an open mouth for the sailors to toss Jonah overboard? By no means! Jonah had testified that his God Jahweh made both the sea and the sky, including all the elements that make them up.

You can trust it. God has made everything in the world, and controls it every moment. The Lord even orders his great creatures to serve a disobedient servant so that he can later be used.

The Lord had prepared this fish to swallow up Jonah. What worse fate could you imagine than being swallowed into the belly of a dank, dark, slimy, writhing fish? You might say Jonah was at the end of the line. He could not sink much lower. He is like Joseph in Pharaoh's prison, only worse. Joseph was an innocent man. But Jonah was guilty, deserving death for refusing to show the compassion of the Lord toward others.

'And Jonah was in the belly of the fish three days and three nights' (*Jon. 1:17b*).

Some people have proposed that Jonah actually died in the belly of the fish. We do not know, but it is at least possible. God then would have raised him from the dead after three days. Clearly God's intent in Jonah's experience was to represent the prophet as rising to a life of service to God after sinking down to death in disobedience.

Why the three days? Something in the order of

[29]

things dictated the three days. If such a fate can be put positively, it was not to be more than three days that Jonah would be in the belly of the fish. For three days he was to rest in the bottom of the sea, as though death were being confirmed. But it must be only for three days. Then he must be brought up from the abyss.

The same divine sense of timing is also present in the third-day offering of Isaac. In Abraham's heart, his only beloved son had been as good as dead from the moment the two of them departed for Mt. Moriah. Abraham held in his heart the commitment to offer Isaac as a sacrifice on the mountain specified by the Lord. On the third day it was as though he had received Isaac back from the dead. And remember: Mt. Moriah is the same as Mt. Zion, where the sacrifices at the temple in Jerusalem later were offered for hundreds of years.

Jesus Christ finally was offered on the neighbouring hill of Golgotha. Paul says that Christ was raised from the dead on the third day according to the Scriptures (*I Cor. 15:4*). After being humiliated through his subjection to the powers of death long enough to confirm that he really was dead, he came up from the abyss.

'So Jonah prayed to Jahweh his God' (*Jon. 2:1*).

There is no indicator that Jonah had prayed earlier at the direction of the captain of the ship. The captain had said, 'Cry to your god'. He used a word that describes a prayer of desperation. 'Cry out' – with the most intense sense of anguish and anxiety. The ship sinks. We have little or no hope. Scream above the sounds of the storm until your God hears!

While on the deck of the tossing ship, Jonah apparently did not pray. His conscience restrained him. He was not at the point of repentance. Not until he was ready to do the Lord's will in going to Nineveh was he able to pray.

Do you sometimes have trouble praying? It may be that your conscience restrains you. Unconfessed sin is like a fishbone caught in the windpipe. You cannot breathe with any semblance of normality until you remove the obstruction.

Are you alienated from a brother, or running from doing the will of God? It will affect your prayer life drastically. You will shrivel in your soul from a lack of vital communion with the Lord.

But finally Jonah prays. Jonah prays to the Lord from the bowels of the fish.

What can you learn from this locale of Jonah's prayer? You can learn that even from the point of chastening you may pray to the Lord. When you are in the deepest depths, you still may call on him.

> 'And he said:
>   "I cried out
>   from my distress to Jahweh
>   And he answered me;
>   from the belly of sheol
>   I cried for help;
>   You heard my voice"'
>
> (*Jon. 2:2*)

There is such a thing as an imagined distress. Like Ichabod Crane in the *Legend of Sleepy Hollow*, men may imagine that disaster is in hot pursuit when in reality it is not.

[31]

But whatever your actual circumstance, cry out to the Lord whenever you think you need help. The Lord will hear and deliver even from imaginary dangers.

When real distress in life comes, cry out with a full earnestness. He will hear, answer and deliver.

> '"For you had cast me
>> into the deep,
>> in the heart of the seas;
>> and the river
>>> surrounded me.
>> All your breakers
>> and your waves
>>> passed over me"'
>> (*Jon. 2:3*)

Jonah has no problem identifying the Lord as the 'prime mover' of his distress. God is the one who had cast him into the sea, although the sailors actually did the deed. It was not the ocean as some inanimate 'it' or a personified 'she' that posed the threat to his very life. These were God's waves and breakers that were threatening to swallow him.

A person can develop a paranoia by seeing God everywhere and in everything, if it is not done with a proper faith. But it must be recognized that God is in control of all, and all the various elements of the world must be seen as subject to him. You are never abandoned into a world of irrational chance. You remain under the superintendence of the sovereign Lord of heaven and earth.

'And as for me, I said:
> "I am cast out
>> from before your eyes;

[32]

Ahh! I shall look again
  to your holy temple"'

(Jon. 2:4)

Jonah recognizes the genuine peril of his condition. It is not merely that he is experiencing physical calamity; his soul has been cast off by his God.

Try to imagine the terrors of being hurled from the deck of a ship into those massive, swirling waves. What would it be like to be pounded to the verge of unconsciousness while being submerged into the salty sea? Then you awaken in pitch blackness, in the slimy pit of the fish's belly. You are heaved back and forth by the perpetual motion of the great sea creature. You know yourself to be among the damned at the bottom of the abyss, dwelling in outer darkness. Jonah had wanted to escape the presence of God. Now he experienced a slight taste of the fulfilment of his wish.

Having realized his situation, what does Jonah do? He recognizes that he has been banished from the presence of God. But he nonetheless turns to God's most holy place.

What boldness! What audacity! Cannot he see that he is totally unworthy to approach the holy place of the Lord? Doesn't the judgment of God on his life indicate that he ought to turn inward to himself rather than outward to the Lord?

If a sinning, selfish, loveless, disobedient servant of the Lord under the Old Testament has such boldness in approaching the very God he has offended, how much more should you approach the throne of grace with boldness? When you are

[33]

suffering severe chastening from the Lord, admit your wrong and return to him. There you must leave your case. The last thing you want to do is turn inward on yourself and despair. Look up! Look far, far away to the dwelling-place of the Lord. Apply to the objective benefits that can be found in his sovereign mercy alone.

When you observe the way the Lord treated his servant Jonah, you can surely hope. Be ready to turn whenever you stray, whenever you are chastened. Come with a new commitment to submit this time to the Lord's will. Put your entire trust in the mercy of God as it is found in the death of Jesus Christ for rebellious sinners.

Jonah's look of hope from the pit has a very specific object. It is not God in the abstract to which he looks. It is not to the calculated odds that his fortunes will turn. It is to the holy temple of the Lord that he looks. During Jonah's earlier ministry in the days of Jeroboam II, the northern kingdom had expanded its holdings back to the borders of the days of Solomon. But Jonah was wise enough not to equate material prosperity with acceptability by God. He looked not to Samaria, but to the temple in Jerusalem, the capital of the southern kingdom of Judah. There he saw the place of his hope.

Jonah knew of the sacrifices being offered in Jerusalem. Although he was a prophet of the northern kingdom, he knew that his hope was at the altar of that one place on earth designated by God for the reconciliation of sinners to himself.

That one place of reconciliation now is the earthly Jerusalem only in an historical sense. No pilgrimages to the city, no imaginary approaching of the old temple is the way of life for the sinner. Now you have a new and living way into the real 'holy place' which is in heaven. By faith in the sacrifice of Jesus Christ, you may approach the heavenly Jerusalem. There you will find God reigning in power with sovereign grace. It is the one place in the universe where the sinner may be reconciled to God.

Do not despair. Do not give in to a sense of despondency and hopelessness. You are certainly not as far gone as Jonah. You may *think* God has cast you off, but Jonah *knew* he was. You may feel you are in the pits, but Jonah had been three days in the pitch-black slime of the fish's belly. You may fear you have missed God's will for your life, but Jonah understood perfectly well that he was the wilful rebel on the run.

Yet he looked to the Lord.

So can you. Do it right now. Before you move one inch. Stop fidgeting in your seat. Do not wait to set things right before you come to the Lord any more than did Jonah. Turn your heart and your eyes to the Lord. Then he will come with his salvation.

> "'The waters
>   engulfed my very life,
> The abyss
>   enclosed me;
> Seaweed
>   entwined my head.
> To the uttermost foundations of the
>   mountains
>   I sunk;

[35]

The earth with her bars
    placed me in perpetual confinement"'

(Jon. 2:5, 6a)

Jonah was a most successful prophet. But you would not want to be like Jonah in every respect. You would not want to track Jonah's career every step of the way.

But one man did. The waters engulfed his very life. The abyss enclosed him. God forsook this other man, and he descended into hell. The stone enclosed him in the tomb, and for three days he remained silently in the grave where his body rested.

All praise to Jesus Christ the suffering servant of the Lord! He endured things worse than Jonah. Hell itself was his cup to drink, not merely a mouthful of salt water. The Lord pursued Jonah to the point of death for the sake of the salvation of many, but he pursued Christ to the fact of hell to save numberless sinners throughout the history of the world.

'"But you brought up my life from destruction,
    O Jahweh my God;
When my soul was exhausted within me,
    I remembered
        Jahweh,
    and my prayer came
        to you,
        to your holy temple"'

(Jon. 2:6b–7)

Have you ever asked the question, Why did the Lord bother with Jonah? Why did he not simply find another servant to do the job?

[36]

God brought Jonah back so that the prophet himself might be a sign. His life would embody the message he preached. Jonah's life testified to the fact that God judged a sinner without partiality, found him guilty, and cast him into the watery abyss. But from this abyss, the Lord lifted a guilty, condemned sinner to life and service. The sign of Jonah proclaims the gospel truth about the justice and the mercy of God.

When Jonah finally went to preach in Nineveh, why should the people believe him? Why should they pay attention to another crackpot shouting with a strange accent in their streets? Times Square is full of these kinds of people.

Jonah had to be believed because he himself was a sign. His life-experience testified to the facts. God in righteousness judges sin to the point of death. God in mercy restores the sinner to life and service.

The sign of today is the sign of Jonah. 'No sign will be given this generation except the sign of Jonah,' said Jesus to the Pharisees (*Matt. 12:39*). Jonah's sign declares the impartiality of God's judgment and the gracious miracle of resurrection from the dead.

Today the message of the sign of Jonah has been intensified by the death and the resurrection of Jesus Christ. His death shows that no salvation is possible other than through the substitution of Christ's suffering the righteous judgment of God in the place of sinners. His resurrection displays the sure hope of new life and service for sinners united by faith to him.

Resurrection hope centres on the Lord. Man

[37]

cannot deliver himself from the coming calamity of divine judgment. Only looking to the supernatural power of the Lord, crying out to him, directing your petitions to the point of his resurrection power can deliver from spiritual and physical death. As Charles Wesley has expressed it in his resurrection hymn:

Christ the Lord is risen today, Alleluia!
Sons of men and angels say; Alleluia!
Raise your joys and triumphs high; Alleluia!
Sing, ye heavens, and earth, reply; Alleluia!

Soar we now where Christ has led, Alleluia!
Following our exalted head; Alleluia!
Made like him, like him we rise; Alleluia!
Ours the cross, the grave, the skies. Alleluia!

> '"Those who cling
>   to falsifying vanities
>   their hope of mercy
> They have abandoned.
>
> But I with a voice of thanksgiving
>   will sacrifice to you;
> That which I have vowed
>   I will surely fulfil.
> SALVATION IS FROM JAHWEH!"'
>   (*Jon. 2:8, 9*)

In these last words of his resurrection poem, Jonah reflects on the nature of true faith. For only true faith in Jahweh can deliver from the chastening hand of the God of heaven, earth, the sea and the sky. Learn from the sign of Jonah the lessons of true faith:

[38]

First, true faith clings to the Lord even when he is chastening you. It is like a child riding the merry-go-round. The faster the merry-go-round spins, the tighter the child clings. A person with true faith cries out to the Lord even as he sinks into the abyss.

Secondly, true faith offers a perpetual sacrifice of thanks to the Lord. In the belly of the fish, Jonah hardly could offer anything else. But his sacrifice was no less acceptable. For it is not things that God desires, but the loyalty of the heart.

Thirdly, true faith manifests itself in keeping its word. Once Jonah was released from the fish, he headed for Nineveh. He had made a vow to the Lord, and faith led him to keep it.

You too have vowed to the Lord. As a believer, you have said you would live as a Christian. You have vowed to support the Lord's church. You have committed yourself to turn from sin and walk in the light of the Lord. Keep your word as a way of manifesting the true character of your faith.

Fourthly, true faith recognizes that all salvation comes from the Lord. He alone and no other can save. No one else has descended into the abyss of hell for sinners but Jesus Christ. Salvation is from the Lord, and from the Lord alone.

'And the Lord spoke to the fish, and it vomited Jonah on the dry land' (*Jon. 2:10*).

That is all God has to do. He spoke at creation, and all the world came into being. He speaks again, and sinners are redeemed. Whatever your need, calamity, disobedience or dilemma – God must speak for you. Then everything will turn to your good.

[39]

When God speaks to the fish, instantly Jonah is transposed from the dank, dark belly of the fish to the brilliant beauty of the Riviera. The creature that had been a dungeon for him now becomes Jonah's free transport to the beach. The fish drops him off at the seaside, and Jonah basks on the pleasant beaches of the Mediterranean.

Who knows? Perhaps this little breather on the beach was the time that Jonah composed this poem that now constitutes the second chapter of his book.

Life can be poetic for you. Whatever your distress, you can look to the temple of the Lord. Turn to the perfect sacrifice of Christ on behalf of your sins, and your life will be transformed from the abyss to the bounties of God's blessing. Turn to him now with a new faith and a renewed intent to do his will. Then you will enjoy the newness of resurrection life in Christ.

4

COMMISSION
(Jonah 3:1–10)

We have a story to tell to the nations. Our story has greater potential for helping a troubled world than all the proposals of the politicians of all the nations.

Our message comes from the third chapter of the book of Jonah. But its greatest summary is found in the last chapter of the book of Luke. Jesus, like Jonah, had rested three days in the belly of the earth. Jesus, like Jonah, came forth with a commission for reaching the world. Listen again to the words of the resurrected Lord, and note how his commission parallels the command given Jonah 800 years earlier. The theme is repentance and the remission of sins. The passage is Luke 24:45–49:

45 Then he opened their minds so they could understand the Scriptures. 46 He told them, 'This is what is written: The Christ will suffer and rise from the dead on the third day, 47 and repentance and forgiveness of sins will be preached in his name to all nations, beginning at Jerusalem. 48 You are witnesses of these things. 49 I am going to send you what my Father has promised; but stay in the city until you have been clothed with power from on high.'

Now consider how this commission of Christ had its foreshadowing in the book of Jonah.

[41]

'And the word of Jahweh came to Jonah the second time' (*Jon. 3:1*).

How wonderful! God says, Let's go at it again. The wording of this new commission to Jonah is virtually identical with the wording of his original charge. Let's start from the first, says the Lord. Let's forget about the past, and act as though it never happened.

God forgets, and never holds the thing against you. Think of how wonderful are the implications of that one fact for your life. God simply does not hold grudges against people who humble themselves and ask his forgiveness through Jesus Christ.

Men have a much greater problem forgiving and forgetting than does God. You may discover that you have a very difficult time forgetting your mistakes of the past. But God does not have that kind of trouble.

One popular television programme does nothing but replay bloopers. It is all in good humour, and everyone enjoys the notoriety of being human. Everybody enjoys such humour . . . but only because the programme is very selective. It never displays the really notorious bloopers. It does not show temperamental actors cursing and shouting at their directors.

Sometimes politicians make a career for themselves by exhuming rotten corpses of the past. They convince themselves that they have the right to demand perfection of sinful, fallible human beings. But all the time they hope no one will catch them at their own mistakes.

But God is different. You would not know he were different if it were not for the Christian gospel. For nothing can remove the condemnatory memory of the past but the blood of Jesus Christ.

Jonah's experience is a sign, a parable of the forgiveness and the grace of God. He ran from God, refusing to show the Lord's love and compassion. God pursued him to the death, walled him in, led him to genuine repentance, and restored him to service.

Are you running from the will of God for your life? The Lord may come to you the second time. He may let you start all over again, offering to use you in his service. Be sure you are ready when that glorious moment comes. Do not be crippled by pride that refuses to admit past mistakes, or their gravity. Unless like Jonah you are willing to admit your sin, the Lord may pass you over.

'"Arise, go to Nineveh that great city and cry out to it the word which I am telling to you"' (*Jon. 3:2*).

Little distinctions in the Hebrew Bible often mean a lot. Jonah's new commission is almost exactly the same as the first one God gave him. But the change of one letter makes all the difference. On the first occasion, God told Jonah to cry out *against* the city. Now God tells him to cry out *to* the city.

It is not that God has changed his mind. Jonah must still begin with the same message of judgment, denouncing their sin. But Jonah's own experience in and out of the belly of the great fish speaks about the possibility of forgiveness, restoration and blessing after divine condemnation. Jonah now is capable of conveying no other message whether he wished to or not. No matter what he says, his life-experience shouts to his hearers, 'Look at me! Forgiveness and restoration are possible even for those who disobey and run away from God.' Instead of preaching exclusively against the city, Jonah's very presence was a message of hope *to* the city.

Your message as a forgiven sinner should strike the same note just as loudly. Tell people by your attitude toward them that God's love and forgiveness are freely offered through Jesus Christ.

> *Tell me the story of Jesus,*
> *Write on my heart every word;*
> *Tell me the story most precious,*
> *Sweetest that ever was heard.*
>
> *Tell of the cross where they nailed him,*
> *Writhing in anguish and pain;*
> *Tell of the grave where they laid him,*
> *Tell how he liveth again.*
>
> *Love in that story so tender,*
> *Clearer than ever I see:*
> *Stay, let me weep while you whisper,*
> *Love paid the ransom for me.*
>
> *Fanny J. Crosby*

Are you beginning to get the full picture of Jonah's commission? God let Jonah run. He ordered Jonah's life just so that it would anticipate the gracious ministry of the Lord Jesus Christ. Both Jonah and Jesus descend into the abyss. For three days they lie in the enclosures of death. Then God speaks, their graves swing open, and they carry out a commission of gospel proclamation to the whole world. The Gospel of Luke says that Christ died and was raised on the third day 'according to the Scriptures.' Then Luke presents Christ commanding his disciples to preach repentance and remission of sins to the nations. This glorious proclamation was to be done in the power of the abiding Holy Spirit. He would give his disciples the words they should say moment by moment and day by day.

Jonah's second commission sounds the same. He is to declare exactly the words that God will be saying to him.

You live in the era of the One greater than Jonah. Having come out of the tomb, the resurrected Christ tells you to go to all the nations and declare his forgiveness. You, like Jonah, are to speak the words he will be telling you as the indwelling Holy Spirit opens his word to you.

'So Jonah arose and went into Nineveh according to the word of Jahweh. Now Nineveh was a very large city [or, a city greatly significant to God], a walk of three days' (*Jon. 3:3*).

Now Jonah is on the move. He is reaching out to the masses of men. He is fulfilling the great commission.

Be fully aware that you have this same responsibility. By life and by word you are to embody the principle of God's call to repentance and faith, reaching out to the multitudes in need.

Be sure you do not make a mistake as you universalize Jonah's commission. When God sends Jonah to the big city, it is not that he intends to ignore the little towns and villages of the earth. Jesus and his disciples went through all the villages and towns spreading the gospel. If the church growth movement intends to reach out with missionary effort only to the large metropolitan cities of the world, it is in serious error. The great commission explicitly says that the church is to go into all the world and preach the gospel to every creature.

This famous three-day walk of Jonah need not have been straight through the city, or directly around the city. It could have involved a criss-cross pattern touching all the major sections of the city. In any case, it was a large and significant city with a desperate need for the gospel.

This city of Nineveh actually was not much different from the modern metropolis. Zig-zag through your own city if you will. Some sections you will not feel comfortable entering day or night. Others may seem intimidating because of the wealth, the intellect and the political power that is present. Yet the whole of the city needs the message Jonah brought to Nineveh.

Who among us is commissioned by God to fulfil some part of this assignment? Better yet, which of us does not have a part to play? We have a story to tell to the nations.

'And Jonah began to enter the city a walk of a single day. He cried out loudly, saying: "Yet forty days and Nineveh shall be overthrown"' (*Jon. 3:4*). Walking up and down like a street vendor, Jonah begins to declare the coming destruction of the city.

How did he reach the conclusion that this disaster would come in 40 days? He must have been given that information by the Lord. The only way he could prophesy so specifically about the future was to have a direct revelation from the Lord.

Three things you should remember about this kind of prophecy today. First, do not wait around for a special word from the Lord to determine your role in the great commission. Begin to do now all you can to fulfil the commands of the Lord as they are found so clearly in the Scriptures. Secondly, all the inspired prophecies written in the Bible about the saving of a multitude from every nation shall be fulfilled with or without your aid. This gospel shall indeed be declared to all the nations, and then shall the end come (*Matt. 24:14*). But you have the great privilege of spreading the gospel wherever you are and with whatever gifts you have. Thirdly, understand the completeness of the present era in God's plan as it relates to prophetic revelations. All the prophetic specifics you need for concrete action as Christ's witness are found in the written word of God. Do not cripple your prospects as a witness by leaning on the false expectation of a further, more definite word from the Lord that would direct your efforts. Ask him in faith for wisdom to decide how to use your gifts, and then do what is in your heart.

You don't need more confirming revelation. What you need is more boldness like Jonah. You need his grace to enable you to declare God's coming judgment publicly and unequivocally.

Jonah's message on this occasion sounds like one that might be delivered by a 'kook' today. But remember: he had been in and out of the belly of a great fish. He knew first-hand the reality of God's judgment on sinners. The Lord told him about the future in a way that had been confirmed by his own experience.

You do not need to enter the belly of a great fish

to know the reality of God's judgment on the disobedient. The experience of Jonah and Jesus are enough. If it took the death of the Son of God to make salvation possible, the reality of God's judgment on sin is a certainty. If Jonah and Jesus both were delivered from the pit, you know the certainty of God's mercy to sinners. God delivered Jonah from the grip of death. He raised Jesus Christ from the tomb for the benefit of sinners. Grace is freely offered to men already under the sentence of condemnation from God.

'And they believed God, these men of Nineveh; they cried out for a fast, and put on sackcloth, from the greatest to the least' (*Jon. 3:5*).

How amazing! They believed God!

Do you remember the first time you sold a glass of lemonade at the stand in front of your house? You had painted your sign, set up your table, and sat in the sun for an hour or two. No customers. Then this nice lady from next door actually came over, thought about the choices you offered, and gave you a dime for the drink. You rushed inside shouting, 'Momma, Momma, I sold my first drink. Look! A real dime!' You had hoped to sell something, but you were overwhelmed when it really happened.

Jonah must have felt the same way. He must have been stunned when more and more people indicated that they actually believed him!

But why should you be surprised when people come to faith in Christ? Don't you realize that the prouder, the more sinful people are, the more miserable they are? Did God not give his only Son to save sinners? Isn't the Holy Spirit real, causing men to be born again?

From the greatest to the least the people of Nineveh believed God. The down-and-outers and the up-and-outers alike responded to the message.

The gospel is no respecter of persons. It has the power to save the hippies and the yuppies. It speaks equally to the power-brokers of politics as well as the dealers in drugs.

The Bible says the people of Nineveh believed *God*, not Jonah. It was not the force of the argument presented by the prophet that moved the people. It was the power of God's truth that pierced to the heart. Never rely on your own persuasive powers as the way to save sinners. Never wait until you have confidence in yourself to speak up for Christ. It is God and his truth that people believe. You must remain only the instrument.

'The message smote the king of Nineveh. He got up from his throne, set aside his robe of royalty, covered himself with sackcloth, and collapsed in the dust' (*Jon. 3:6*).

Like an unexpected stroke, the word of Jonah crushed the heart of the king. The truth of God contains within itself the power to cut directly through every human rationalization.

Have you seen the painting of the man with his hand covering one eye while the other eye stares out in stunned horror? Sometimes God's word smites a person so that it has just that kind of effect. Never despair over any person's salvation. When God speaks to him, he will be shaken to his very core.

Don't be sceptical over this report of the power of

the word of God in the life of the heathen king of Nineveh. It is happening all the time. It is going on today. Look at Chuck Colson. God's word pierced his arrogant heart, and he collapsed before its power. The important thing for you is to be out there where people are, telling them the message. You have a story to tell to the nations that shall turn their hearts to the right.

'Then he cried out in Nineveh: "In accord with the taste [Heb. *taam*] of the king and his great ones, neither man nor beast nor cattle nor flock shall taste [Heb. *taam*] a thing. No one shall eat or even drink water. They shall be covered with sackcloth, both man and beast, and shall cry out to God with all their might. Let each and every man turn from his evil ways and from the violence which he has inflicted with his own hands. Who knows whether or not God also will turn and be moved in compassion? Then he might turn from his rage and we will not perish"' (*Jon. 3:7–9*).

God have compassion? Where did the king of Nineveh get that idea? Not from his own concept of God, to be sure. Neither did he get the idea of God's compassion from his own dealings with other people. Archaeology records that the kings of Nineveh regularly cut off the noses of the people they conquered, and literally skinned them alive.

Where did this heathen king get the idea that God might have compassion if he repented of his sin? Why, from Jonah, of course. Despite himself, Jonah embodied the message that God was compassionate. He was in himself a sign of God's grace. He ran from the will of God, and yet was brought out alive from the belly of the great fish. The king of

Nineveh took courage every time he looked at Jonah. Perhaps there might be compassion from God for the sinners of Nineveh as well.

The story of Jonah is a great one. It has captured people's imagination for hundreds of years. But the story you have been commissioned to tell is not only about Jonah. It is about a greater than Jonah. The story you tell the nations is about the death of Jesus Christ for sinners, and his resurrection from the dead on the third day. You speak not only of death but of resurrection. Your message not only is of the judgment of God for sinners, but of his mercy as well.

If it were not for Christ's resurrection, your message would be exclusively of judgment. The death of Christ without his resurrection would be a dead end street, offering no hope beyond the present life. But his coming alive declares plainly that God intends to bless men throughout this life and into eternity. No matter how severe may be his chastening judgments, men always have the possibility of a way back to salvation and life. Beyond the 'light afflictions' you endure now are the realities of eternity with loved ones and with Christ forever.

It is startling to see the mercy of God toward Jonah. That man deliberately ran from the will of God. He showed no more love to others than a hardened granite stone. Why then should God love him? At the bottom of the sea was where he belonged.

But God raised him up.

Now the love of God is extended to the king of Nineveh, his leaders and all his people. How could it be? They were far worse than Jonah. They did not merely run from the will of God, they brutalized the nations of the earth. The king himself readily admits that brutality is the sin for which they must repent. God sees their repentance, and he turns from his decree of judgment:

'And God saw their deeds; for they turned from their evil ways. So God had compassion. Concerning the evil that he had said he would do to them, he did not do it' (*Jon. 3:10*).

God saw not only what they said but what they did. Their faith produced works. So he showed love to them and spared them from the destruction he had announced.

How merciful is your God! The resurrection of Christ and his subsequent commission says, 'Whosoever will, let him come.' No matter what a man's record of running from God or of brutality toward man, he may find God's mercy and compassion.

Go into all the world and declare the good news to every creature. And whoever repents and turns to the Lord with a faith that produces good works shall be saved.

The story of Jonah is a great one. But greater than the story of Jonah is the story of Jesus. It is this story that we tell to the nations.

Are you telling the story? Telling it to all the world? That is your commission.

5

COMPASSION

(Jonah 4:1–11)

The book of Jonah may be summarized in one word: compassion. The centrality of compassion does not become explicit until this last chapter. But that is the way a good story often unfolds. Now feel the impact of the total message of the book of Jonah by considering the theme of compassion.

'But it was a very evil thing to Jonah, and he became angry' (*Jon. 4:1*).

What was a very evil thing to Jonah? The phrase refers to the last verse of the preceding chapter: 'When God saw what they did and how they turned from their evil ways, he had compassion' (*Jon. 3:10*). That was the evil thing to Jonah! God's compassion!

Often the best teaching is done by contrast. You appreciate the speed of an Olympic runner when you see him or her leave the pack behind. You see the greatness of God's compassion to the Ninevites when you set it beside Jonah's reaction. God loved and cared for these wicked Ninevites, just as he does for the cruel, brutal drug-dealers of today. Indeed, he expects repentance and trust; but he stands ready to receive the most wicked of the earth.

Most translations say this compassion of the Lord was 'greatly displeasing' to Jonah. But the more straightforward translation is that Jonah saw a 'great evil' in this forgiveness by the Lord. How could he see it otherwise? The Assyrians were an extremely vicious people. They had done permanent damage to nations all over the world. How then could God so readily forgive them for the evil they had done? Had not David the man after God's own heart been required to suffer for his sin of adultery and murder all his life? Is not this compassion of the Lord a manifestation of 'cheap grace'?

So Jonah was angry. He was a man of passion. He may not have had much compassion, but he had plenty of passion. Often younger men have more passion than compassion. James and John in their earlier days were known as the sons of thunder. They were ready to call down fire from heaven on the Samaritans who would not receive Jesus (*Lk. 9:54*). But later in life, the beloved John writes more about the love of God than any of the other disciples.

Young Christians, beware of an excessive zeal that tends to run over the feelings of people. All doctrine is meant to lead us to holiness, and if your doctrine makes you insensitive to people, then you probably do not understand the doctrine correctly. Be very careful about justifying your anger as 'righteous indignation', or your impatience as zeal for the truth. Love is the all-encompassing truth, and patience is the first fruit of love. 'So he prayed to Jahweh and said, "Ahh, Jahweh! Is not this exactly what I said would happen while I was still in my homeland? That is why I got up so quickly to flee to Tarshish. I have known that you are: (1) a God of mercy and compassion, (2) slow to arrive at anger, (3) full of love, and (4) constantly turning away from inflicting evil"' (*Jon. 4:2*).

Jonah had it all right from the beginning. There was no question about it. He could not be faulted for his understanding of the nature of God. As a matter of fact, it was this insight that had led him originally to run from the Lord.

The key to understanding Jonah's reaction to the Lord's compassion is found in one little word in the original text, 'my homeland'. While I was at home, on my own territory, in association with my own people, then I had this insight about what would happen in this other place where you wanted to send me.

The prophet of the Lord manifests the worst sort of provincialism. God's land is his land, God's people his people, God's customs his customs. Oh yes, God may work elsewhere with other people under other circumstances. In his generosity, Jonah will allow for that possibility. But in so far as he is concerned, only his God and his people go together.

Generally provincialism is associated with country towns, rural areas, isolated mountain communities. But provincialism can be felt just as strongly in metropolitan areas. One great map of New York city shows the cluster of islands weighted down with skyscrapers prominently filling most of the picture. The rest of America is shrunk to a comparatively small section that is labelled 'The Wilderness'.

Provincialism is in us all. From one perspective, a sense of belonging to a particular area and group

[55]

is important. But it can be overdone. It becomes sin when somehow other peoples are viewed as not being proper recipients of the mercy of God.

All through the ages, people and nations have claimed for themselves a favourable position before God. Charlemagne claimed this role for the 'holy Roman empire.' John Milton claimed it for England. Numerous people have claimed it for the United States of America.

It is true that God sometimes grants special privileges, blessings and favours to certain nations and peoples at different times. Why the Lord makes these distributions he does not explain to us. We should joyfully receive every grace he shows to us and our land with thanksgiving and praise.

The problem arises when by attitude or action we pull back from the people richer or poorer than we, those more educated or less educated than we, those that live farther to the North, the South, the East or the West than we. Then we become guilty of closing our heart of compassion. Then we have ceased to reflect the heart of Christ.

'"So now, O Jahweh, take my life from me; for it is better to die than to live"' (*Jon. 4:3*).

What has got into him? Is he simply exhausted from the emotional exertion of preaching throughout the city?

No, Jonah is reacting to what he sees to be the inevitable. His people the Israelites, the inhabitants of his precious homeland, had not repented for over one hundred and fifty years. Yet the Ninevites repent in a day. The conclusion seems obvious. The centre of gravity for God's working in the world must be shifting. He is going to include in the blessings of redemption the vast hordes of the Gentile world!

So Jonah does not want to live to see it. In one sense, he is like the Apostle Paul, who was willing to have himself cursed for the sake of his people the Israelites. But in another sense he is nothing like Paul. He does not wish to be a missionary to the Gentile world as was Paul if prophetic success eventually will put Israel in a second-place role. He cannot stand to witness the addition of foreigners to the number of the people of God if it means the Lord's judgment on his kinsmen.

Jonah has another concern. It depresses him that mercy should be shown so generously to a people as brutal and as wicked as the Ninevites. He cannot find it in his heart to forgive them as does the Lord.

Have you forgiven the person at work that knifed you in the back? Have you forgiven the relative who borrowed money and never repaid you? Have you a heart to forgive the teacher who brought your precious child to tears? Study the compassion of God, and use it as the measuring rod that will tell you when to forgive.

'Then Jahweh said, "Are you reacting properly to show such anger?"' (*Jon. 4:4*).

How tender and patient is the Lord with Jonah! First Jonah runs from doing the Lord's will. Then he repents, confesses his wrong, and starts on the right path. He will preach to the Ninevites.

Yet now we learn that all the time he was doing the Lord's will, he was begrudging the activity. He

[57]

never really had made his desires one with the
Lord's. He was the most half-hearted preacher you
have ever seen.

All this time he knew exactly what the Lord
wanted. He knew that the Lord wanted the
Ninevites to repent so that they could be spared.
God loved the Ninevites despite all their sin. He
was rooting for them.

But the last thing Jonah wanted was for the
Ninevites to be spared. Even though he knew it was
the Lord's will, he did not want it.

Do you know the definition of a frustrated
coach? A frustrated coach is one whose quarterback deliberately runs his own play rather than the
coach's. The quarterback knows the coach wants
him to give the ball to the fullback and let him
punch the one yard left to the goal. But for a little
vainglory, the quarterback calls a run-pass option
for himself. In his heart of hearts, the quarterback
is not with the coach.

How could it be that sinful, forgiven human
beings would begrudge God's plan to show mercy
to others? How could Jonah resent God's grace to
the Ninevites after he himself had been restored
from the jaws of death?

'I would never have that attitude,' you say. Yet
every time you are jealous of the blessings, the
talents, the friends, the family of others, you are
expressing resentment at the goodness of God.

'Then Jonah went forth from the city, sat to the
east of the city, and made for himself a booth. He sat
under it in the shade, waiting to see what would
happen to the city' (*Jon. 4:5*).

Do you know what it is like to be out of synch with the Lord? It is a miserable feeling. You can sail along on your arrogance for a while. But ultimately you are miserable. No one who walks out of the will of the Lord for long can remain a very happy person.

Jonah sets up a little camp. He is going to wait out the 39 days until the time has come for the destruction of the city. He is almost daring God not to fulfil the prophetic word of destruction for Nineveh that he has uttered.

Some people stalk through life, breathing out fire and smoke. They intend to pour out their own vengeance on the earth, hastening the day of judgment that God in his compassion has deliberately delayed. Jonah came close to manifesting that very spirit as a result of his intense zeal to protect the well-being of his 'kinsmen according to the flesh' whom he loved so greatly.

'Now Jahweh-Elohim prepared a gourd, and it grew up over Jonah to be a shade for his head to provide shade for him from his evil; and Jonah rejoiced over the gourd with great joy' (*Jon. 4:6*).

Note the hyphenated name for God. In England, the hyphenated name often designates nobility. In the Bible, a combined name for God brings to mind all the various attributes associated with the combination. 'Jahweh' is the God of the covenant, the one who swore with an oath that he would redeem his people. 'Elohim' refers to the God of creative power, the one who speaks and it is done, both in creation and in history.

The combination 'Jahweh-Elohim' first appears with reference to God's placing man in the garden of Eden. The Lord shows his care for man by providing a special environment for him where he may prosper.

Now Jahweh-Elohim shows the same care for Jonah. Burning up in the mid-east sun, Jonah delights in the Lord's provision of a fast-growing vine that supplies cool shade from the tortuous heat.

See the goodness of God! He gives concrete evidence to Jonah that he still regards him with tenderest love. Even though he intends to show mercy to the Ninevites, his love still has plenty of room for Jonah and the Israelites as well.

The Lord deals with Jonah like a parent deals with one child who has become jealous over another. Even as the prophet stares with glaring eyes at the silhouetted city of Nineveh, the loving Father drapes his compassionate arm over the shoulders of Jonah and assures him that he is loved no less for the compassion shown to the repentant city.

Now a greater than Jonah has come. The Lord Jesus looks over Jonah's city of Jerusalem and weeps. Yet his reason for sadness is the exact opposite of Jonah's. 'O Jerusalem, Jerusalem, how often would I have gathered you as a hen gathers her brood, and you would not. So your city is left to you desolate' (*Lk. 13:34, 35*). Jonah grieves that a repentant city shall be spared; Jesus grieves that an unrepentant city must be judged. Jonah laments the prospect of loss for his people that could be brought about by the salvation of heathen sinners; Jesus laments that even the surrendering of his own lifeblood will not bring salvation to Jerusalem.

COMPASSION (JONAH 4:1–11)

What is the condition of your compassion today? Are you more like Jonah or Jesus? Do you wince and draw back every time you are stung when trying to help others? Or do you gladly surrender life itself for the sake of saving people who hurt you? Let the limits of your compassion be determined by Jesus, not Jonah.

'Now the Lord prepared a worm at the break of day on the morrow, and it smote the gourd and it dried up' (*Jon. 4:7*).

Jonah hardly had time to get used to the pleasantness of the shade of this gourd. Then it was gone.

If you think the work of this worm seems exaggerated, try planting some zucchini squash in your garden. A certain bug can get in the stalk of the plant, and overnight the whole beautiful, prolific thing withers and is gone.

Don't turn against the Lord when he looks with disfavour toward you. He may intend to teach many helpful lessons through a little adversity. Remember that instead of a dead gourd, your Lord had the discomfort of a dead tree; and the servant is not greater than his lord.

'Now at the rising of the sun, the Lord prepared a hot east wind, and the sun smote the head of Jonah, and he grew faint to the point that he asked for his soul to die. He said, "It would be better for me to die than to live"' (*Jon. 4:8*).

Four times it is indicated that 'the Lord prepared' something for Jonah. First a fish, then a gourd, then a worm, then a hot east wind. God orders small and great for the good of his prophet,

[61]

and Jonah does not even realize it. Sounds familiar, doesn't it? How many times have you found out later that God had a good purpose going for you that you did not even realize at the time?

Despite all the Lord has prepared for him, Jonah has a death-wish. He is really serious. He is not joking. He wants to die.

Probably if his general circumstances had been different, Jonah would not have been brought to utter despair so quickly. But because he was brooding over the Lord's will for the Ninevites, this little thing of a withered gourd throws him.

Do not minimize the significance of Jonah's heat stroke. Many small calamities will seem just that big to you. They may not be so bad in themselves. But when you are out of kilter with the Lord over his larger purposes for your life, then the lesser things will strike you with greater force. It is like making one miscalculation in your bank account. Once you have made the initial mistake, every piddling payment afterwards will increase your embarrassment ten-fold. The amount may not be much in itself, but it will bring disproportionate trouble.

'Then Elohim said to Jonah, "Was it right for you to be angry over the vine?" "I did right to be angry even to the point of wishing to die," said Jonah. Then Jahweh replied: "*You* had pity on the gourd, over which you did not labour nor did you make it to grow, which was the son of a night, and as the son of a night it perished. And I, should not I have pity on the great city of Nineveh in which there is a multitude of over 120,000 men who do not know their right hand from their left, and also many cattle?"' (*Jon. 4:9–11*).

Compassion is the word – compassion. Jesus was moved with compassion when he saw the multitudes, because they were as sheep without a shepherd (*Matt. 9:36*).

Are you moved with compassion when you see the multitudes? When you commute downtown and see all those people milling about, are you moved with compassion? Do you see beyond their outward form, knowing from the word of God that they are wandering through life aimlessly, not knowing the right perspective on the simplest things of life?

If you must, work yourself through this inspired syllogism on compassion. Move your soul from love of plants to love of animals and then to love of men, as God was trying to do with Jonah.

A gourd, a hanging plant, a tomato vine in your garden. Wouldn't your love for that plant move you if it were mistreated, neglected or trampled? A pet around the house – a dog, a cat, a fish, a bird. You would be concerned if you saw any one of them in distress, would you not?

Transfer that compassion to sinful men. They need your love, just as they need the love of God. Reflect the compassion of Christ toward them.

The book of Jonah ends with a question about compassion. Should not the Lord have had compassion on Nineveh?

How did Jonah answer that question?

We do not know.

So the question remains for you to answer. Compassion! Should not you have a compassion that reflects your Lord's? Considering how graciously he has had compassion on you and yours, should you not show the same compassion toward others? Should not you have compassion even toward sinners that in some ways (but not in all ways) may be worse than yourself?